Contents

Foreword

This booklet has been prepared to show the importance of good siting and sensitive design when building in the countryside. The guidelines which follow will not only help to conserve the landscape, but also they will help to improve the appearance of individual houses without additional cost.

Familiar and successful ways of building from the past are drawn upon and may be applied without inhibiting freedom or imagination in designing new houses for today.

This message is directed at those who may be planning to build their house in the countryside, at designers who need to reconcile the clients' wishes with the need for sensitive development and at the planning authorities who have to decide on the suitability of the siting and design of houses.

The booklet is published by Bord Failte, the Irish Tourist Board, and An Taisce, the National Trust for Ireland, with the co-operation of Galway County Council. It was produced in the Housing and Urban Design Research Unit of the School of Architecture, UCD by Philip Geoghegan, Director, and Delphine Culligan with Eva Byrne and Siobhan Mulcahy. Most of the drawings were made on location in Connemara. The chapter on Planting for Shelter was provided by Richard Webb, An Foras Forbartha.

Introduction

Farmhouse set into landscape and surrounded by shelter planting near Killary Harbour, Co. Galway.

Introduction

Anyone thinking of building a house in the countryside will want the very best designs at an affordable price. In the last twenty years a large proportion of houses built in the countryside look out of place because they were designed as though their appearance in the landscape were unimportant.

Bord Failte with An Taisce are trying to promote good design and siting of houses in the landscape to ensure that Ireland does not end up with more irreparably damaged coastlines or landscapes destroyed by unsympathetic development.

One house in the wrong place, or built out of inappropriate materials can do untold harm to the landscape. On the other hand, thought and care about what may be appropriate need not cost money and should result in a house which will give something to the landscape.

All houses have to be submitted for planning permission and/or approval. The local planning authority will wish to ensure that the building is located in the best place possible and that its form, materials and landscape treatment all help to give it a place and setting in the landscape.

The guidelines for siting and design which follow are meant to give a positive approach and to help in the making of good decisions from the earliest possible stage of a project. They are not absolute as every site will pose particular questions.

It is important therefore to work closely with an architect or designer and to consult with the planning staff of the local authority at an early stage to be sure to obtain the best house possible which fits well into the landscape.

In this way those contemplating building can help to ensure that Ireland's landscapes continue to be a source of delight not only for those who live and work there but also for the visitors for whom they are a major attraction.

Presence and Permanence in the landscape, Leenane, Co. Galway.

Timeless ways of building sensitively

All the clues necessary for building sensitively in the landscape are to be found in the many building traditions within an area. In Connemara, the thatched and whitewashed cottages of the North and the honey-coloured stonework of the South are the earliest examples. But, equally, the classical principles employed in buildings of the nineteenth century provide a good model and guide. There are also many simple and durable houses built in the first half of this century. These all have in common a timeless quality, an inevitability and sense of belonging which gives them presence and permanence in the landscape. They have given the basis for the guidelines.

Building today

Today, building techniques and materials have changed, lifestyle requirements are different, space and comfort expectations are greater.

However, change has inevitably brought with it problems with design; the widespread use of 'pastiche'; copying of suburban bungalows; the use of a riot of materials; inappropriate colours and disrespect for the basic principles of siting and location. However, sensitive and regionally appropriate forms and styles can be used without abandoning the great benefits of technology and twentieth-century developments.

The design guidelines try to set out a basis for a vocabulary, but should not be seen as an opposition to innovation, rather an invitation to be cautious when introducing unfamiliar forms.

It should be emphasised that the design and location of a house is an expert activity, often however carried out without the benefit of professional skills. All house designers are asked to read and observe the simple principles as a starting point for a more sensitive contribution to the environment.

Well-located traditional and modern houses, Sky Road, Clifden, Co. Galway.

Cottage with hipped roof set into the landscape and contained within its garden and shelter planting. Lettergesh, Co. Galway.

Conservation

Whilst the purpose of this booklet is to promote good design in new buildings, the question of caring for old buildings should not be ignored. In many situations it makes more sense financially to upgrade and improve an existing building, and advice from the outset about the potential of an older building could lead to a reconstruction in preference to a new building. Nevertheless, families owning traditional cottages may require new houses more suited to their needs. In such cases every effort should be made to ensure the conservation of the original cottage. Care should be taken in the location of the new dwelling to avoid damage to its existing context, for example, avoiding building behind, in front of, or too close to the original.

The disappearance of traditional cottages especially thatched ones has been rapid in the last decade. Despite the difficulties involved in maintenance and improvement of such dwellings it is a matter for national concern that they have almost completely disappeared.

The disappearance of thatched cottages is a matter of national concern. Lettergesh, Co. Galway.

Locating a house in the landscape

Farmhouse surrounded by shelter planting in the Maam Valley, Co. Galway.

Locating a house in the landscape

The descriptions below characterise the more extreme situations as encountered in Connemara. Nevertheless the principles set out are applicable to gentler landscapes throughout the country.

Types of landscape

Two basic types of landscape are differentiated for the sake of clarity. The first is where the configuration of land beside the sea or inland is hilly, and usually robust enough to contain building. Such a landscape is predominantly a natural one within which buildings occur. The second type is essentially opposite; where landscape is not heavily sloping and where settlement features, buildings and walls, dominate as elements. In this type, it is the buildings, in part at least, which create the landscape.

Low, sheltered farm and yard outside. Clifden, Co. Galway.

Whether buildings sit in or sit on the landscape it is rare that concealment is sought after. It is realistic and necessary to treat buildings as objects in the landscape and consequently to give due attention to their form.

Low-lying inland and coastal areas

Buildings help to form the landscape in low-lying coastal areas. They tend to sit on the land as it is much more difficult to settle them in than in the more hilly landscapes. In addition, shelter-planting may be inhibited by strong and in coastal areas salt-laden winds.

The best examples observed cluster the building elements; house; byres and stores to create sheltered courtyards. Digging-into the landscape also helps to create better aerodynamic conditions to deflect winds and the eventual shelter of trees completes a good local environment.

Traditional cottages frequently tuck into the gentle slope, avoiding the brow and presenting the gable to the exposed windward situation. Retaining walls and boundary walls are also used to define and shelter the house and its local environment.

Simple form tucked into slope with gable to windward.

Hilly and mountainous inland and coastal areas

The contour level is critical to the siting of buildings. In low-lying areas the ground is frequently boggy or poorly drained and liable to flood. The hillsides are steep, exposed and barren. It is therefore the zone between valley-base and hillside which supports habitation, cultivation and pasture; a band along either side of the valley served by an access road. Planting for shelter may be difficult to establish in such areas, yet shelter is all-important to establish wind-free zones around the house and associated buildings. Tree-planting, therefore, is no luxury although it may also serve to enhance the view. It is undertaken in depth to allow for progressive growth and shelter.

Thus the principles of location and siting are no different to those for low-lying areas — shelter being the major determinant of form. However the opportunities are different as are the risks. The contoured landscape produces relatively better situations for exploiting folds in the landscape and gentler slopes are chosen as well as well-drained situations. Thus well-sheltered locations also help the associated shelter-planting to succeed. Houses tend to turn gable and back to the prevailing winds, and to dig into the hillside where the slope allows it.

Newer buildings which do not observe traditional wisdom in siting are strikingly conspicuous in a hilly area. Some of the worst abuses to the landscape can be avoided by the creation and observance of rules about not breaking the skyline and not building on the seaward side of the road.

Houses following the contour-line in the Maam Valley, Co. Galway.

Presence in the landscape

Such a direct response to climate and shelter locates a building in its particular place, settles it into the contours and frames the setting as the shelter planting matures. In their setting houses are neither hidden nor obtrusive. They are surrounded by shelter planting and completed with hedging to the front which gives colour and visual delight as well as a windbreak. Thus it is not only the house but also its associated field patterns, land usage, hedgerows and stone walls which create the landscape.

Houses positioned in this way give a convincing, rational and delightful model for sensitively continuing the process of building and development in Ireland's landscapes.

House in the landscape, Lettergesh, Co. Galway.

Thatched cottage on the Sky Road near Clifden, Co. Galway.

Patterns of houses in the landscape

In many coastal and some inland areas building has occurred at such a density that it is necessary to look not just at the form of the single building but also the way in which all buildings relate to one another. Such patterns need to make sense visually, but more often can be a meaningless, chaotic jumble which ruin the landscape. The development of second homes and holiday homes has contributed markedly to the increase of density in coastal areas, generally with smaller sites used than a house for permanent residence might occupy. In such situations particular care is needed to achieve a visual coherence.

Volumetric similarity of houses and shelter planting reduces the impact of a high density of rural housing, near Killary Harbour, Co. Galway.

Rural and coastal areas in particular are often quite heavily populated with a dispersed and weak settlement structure, creating a number of patterns not really fitting into village or town-type categories. They would include the following:

Scattered houses

There is often a fairly high density of houses with no identifiable pattern of distribution. Their position usually relates to roads and their density depends on the size of agricultural holding. Nevertheless there are good examples of scattered development where the similarity of house-types and the regularity of stone-walls and enclosures succeeds in establishing a form and order in the landscape.

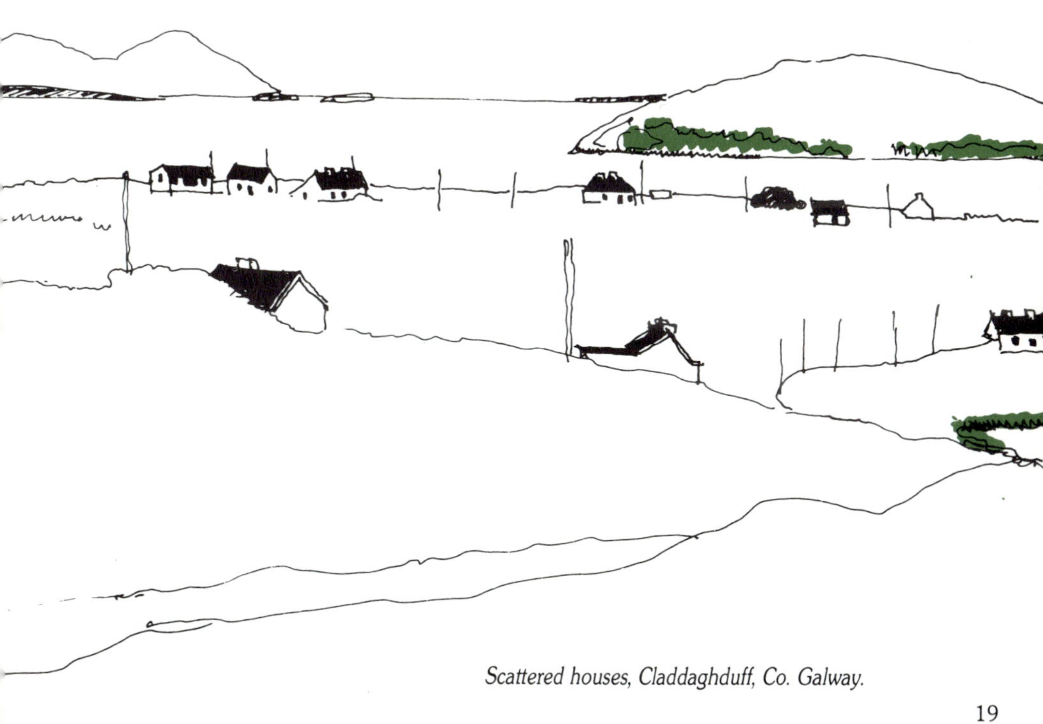

Scattered houses, Claddaghduff, Co. Galway.

Linear development

There are great ranges in the density of settlement from roadside farms separated by stretches of open road to highly intensive ribbon development in scenic areas and outside major settlements. Ribbon development around towns is undesirable and avoidable; it is less easy to pinpoint in coastal rural areas but has a number of undesirable environmental effects. Unbroken lengths of road-side housing obscure real landscape quality as they create a new perceived horizon from the road. Where this occurs between road and coastline it can be disastrous, almost certainly producing a horizon of houses which interrupts sea and beach views and 'inhabiting' the landscape precisely where most travellers would like their views to be uninterrupted.

Random linear development helped by set-back and screening, Claddaghduff, Co. Galway.

Grouped development

Grouped development other than in villages has mainly happened in an accidental way, but may provide a useful model. The groups may be small in number and even with relatively dispersed houses but they read as a group because of the use of similar materials, forms, details and landscape treatment. Excellent traditional examples may still be found in the clachan settlements of South Connemara.

Unfortunately the lessons of these villages are rarely applied but could be incorporated in imaginative planning precepts for new development in areas of higher density building.

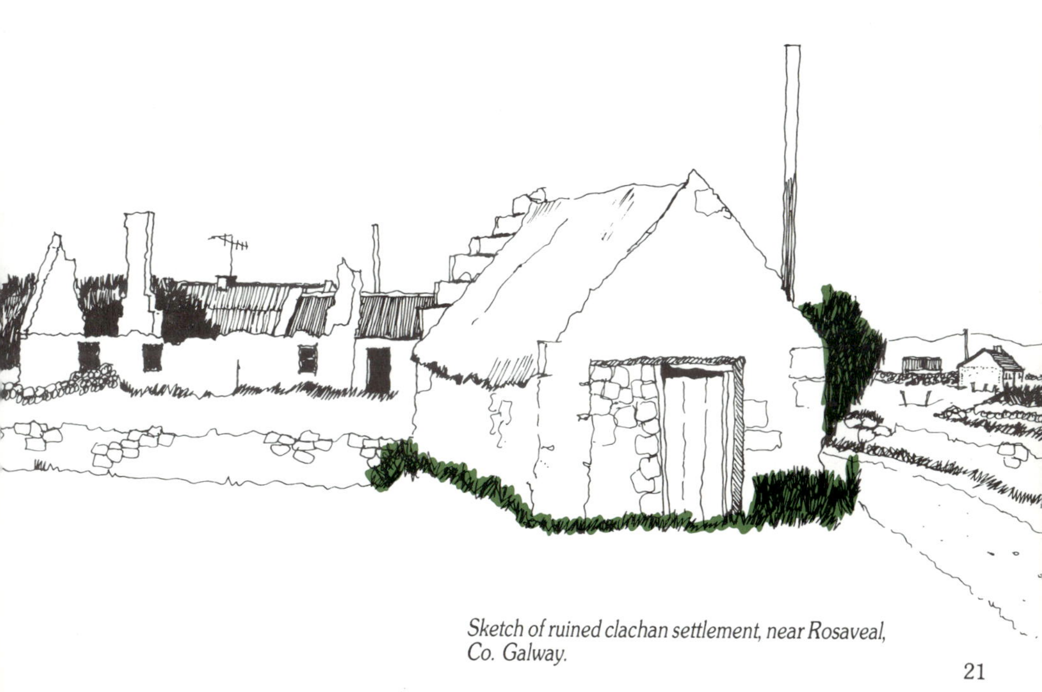

Sketch of ruined clachan settlement, near Rosaveal, Co. Galway.

Design guidelines for locating a house in the landscape

House set in the landscape. Near Killary Harbour, Co. Galway.

Siting principles

Set buildings into their landscape

It is vital to set buildings into their landscape so that they belong when completed. Choosing the gentlest part of a slope, or a naturally occurring shelf, or an indentation or fold, is kinder to the landscape than building on the steepest most prominent part for effect and also optimises shelter.

Respect existing landscape development zones

Along valley-sides there is often a contour level or height where building consistently occurs. New buildings should recognise such existing development zones in the landscape.

Houses set in their landscape. Cashleen, Co. Galway.

Simple forms are most successful, particularly in coastline areas

Buildings are rarely hidden on relatively flat sites, particularly in the coastal landscape. They should be understood as visible objects in the landscape where their form is most important. Simple forms are most successful.

Simple house form in Lettergesh, Co. Galway.

Cut into the hill in preference to filling. Grade fill carefully

In hilly areas, it may be necessary to modify or excavate the landscape before building. It is important that this should not result in excessive scarring. There should be more cutting than fill. Excess fill should be removed or carefully graded, and then planting should be undertaken to settle the building into the landscape.

A. Unsatisfactory visually.
The fill removed from the slope is used to extend the shelf on which the house stands. If the fill is not graded properly the landscape appears scarred and unnatural. The house and its base become a visual intrusion to the slope.

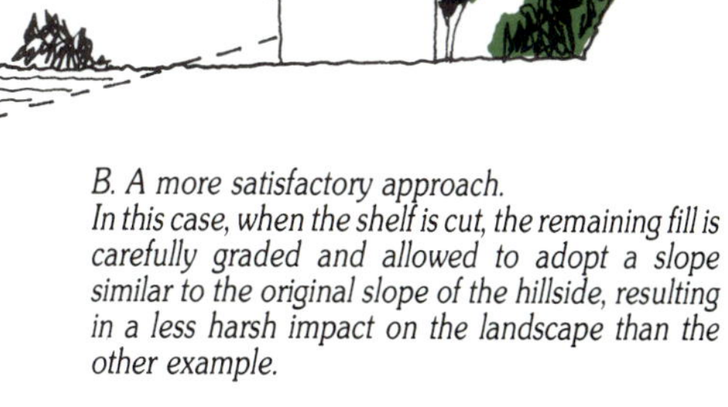

B. A more satisfactory approach.
In this case, when the shelf is cut, the remaining fill is carefully graded and allowed to adopt a slope similar to the original slope of the hillside, resulting in a less harsh impact on the landscape than the other example.

Orientation of the house should recognise prevailing winds, path of the sun and the view

Traditionally, orientation of the house was a matter of prime importance. In view of the high cost of heating there is every reason why it should remain an important element of design. The direction of prevailing winds, micro-climatic conditions, the path of the sun and prospect should be recognised as directives in design.

Landscaping shaped by prevailing winds. Claddaghduff, Co. Galway.

Building should avoid breaking the horizon or water line when seen from the road

Careful control is necessary to keep development off the skyline and to restrict building on the seaward side of the road.

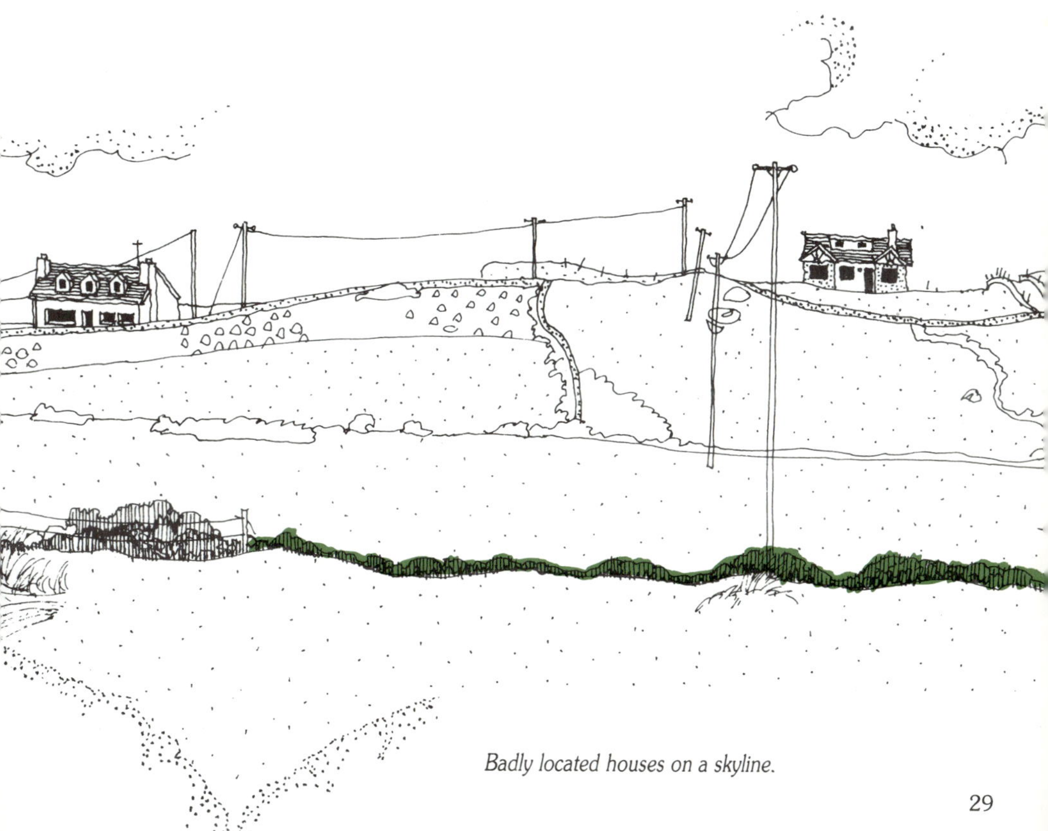

Badly located houses on a skyline.

Access and entry principles

The entrance gateway should announce the building suitably

The entrance gateway announces the building. It is therefore an important element of the design together with the boundary wall. In general, simple treatment of these elements is most successful. The use of stone walls in areas where they are prevalent is desirable in preference to plastered blockwork, or other materials. The conservation of existing stone walls is also important and will help to root new buildings more naturally in the landscape.

Let access road follow contours or cross them gently

The access road should follow contours where possible and cross them gently. It should not read as an ugly gash between gateway and house. Gravel or shale surfaces are kinder on the eye than tarmacadam.

Simple entrance, new stone wall and gentle drive to well-sited new house at Lettergesh, Co. Galway.

Planting principles

Conserve and use the existing landscape to settle and shelter the building

The existing landscape: mature trees, walls, hedges, planting and lanes: is both a resource and a part of the heritage. It should be respected and incorporated when new building takes place, and exploited for its shelter potential.

Use local plant-types to complete landscaping

New planting is usually necessary to complete the incorporation of the building within the existing landscape. The scale of planting should relate to shelter and security needs, and types should be drawn from local planting or after consultation with local nurseries. Chapter 7, 'Planting for Shelter', gives a detailed account of the advantages of shelter planting and the appropriate plant types.

Traditional two-storey farmhouse with shelter planting. Co. Galway.

Clustering and grouping principles

Isolated buildings should complement and not detract from the landscape

Clustered farm buildings. Sky Road, Clifden, Co. Galway.

Isolated buildings should be seen to complement and become part of their landscape. Traditionally ancillary buildings were used to cluster and shelter the house. Their example could be adopted today in design to introduce new ways of emphasising different volumes of the building.

New house organised as a cluster. Claddaghduff, Co. Galway.

New buildings should recognise existing house forms in the landscape

The existing house form in an area, its scale and materials should be observed by designers. This should not stifle innovation; it should be seen as a challenge to use imagination whilst using the language and scale of the existing houses. Forms which are alien to our architectural heritage do not always adapt well and tend to be visually obtrusive to the surrounding landscape.

In densely-built areas, aim for a coherence of pattern and form

In more densely-built areas, development should be guided into coherent patterns by the way houses relate to each other, and by making understandable groupings of houses (e.g. the clachan settlements); unbroken lengths of roadside houses, with competing house-styles create confusion and obstruct the landscape. Unbroken lengths of linear development should be avoided.

Repetition of house form, Lettergesh, Co. Galway.

The form of houses in the landscape

Knockboy, Co. Galway.

The form of houses in the landscape

This section sets out to show that in a given area a knowledge and approach to building has grown which has been successful in a timeless way. Each area has acquired a particular vocabulary to cope with the needs of climate and shelter. Over the years this has become diverse in its expression, as different generations have developed fresh solutions, but despite the diversity there are very clear principles which have not changed. It is something like a language which is constantly added to but which never loses its roots.

The purpose is to encourage those about to undertake building to look around them and learn something of the ways of building which have worked in the past and have come to 'belong' to the countryside or the coast, and to apply the lessons in an enlightened and sensitive way to the problem in hand. Section 2 has set out guiding principles for the siting of houses. This one is complementary in its emphasis on the form and construction of buildings.

Traditional Forms in Inland Areas

The best guide to making shapes that suit the landscape is provided by traditional cottages and farmhouses which have stood the test of time. They are typically single-storey, with long and relatively narrow plans. The houses are one room deep with their room layout apparent from the front. Two-storey houses are prevalent in some areas. They have a narrower frontage, more or less square proportion, with a central door, symmetrical windows on either side and smaller windows on the upper floor.

The roofs are typically pitched at around 45 degrees, mainly with gable-ends, but sometimes with hipped roofs. They are usually very simple in form, occasionally with dormer windows projecting from the roof. The simple, basic form is only extended at the front for the porch.

Ancillary buildings are frequently attached to the side of the main form with the lean-to roof running at right-angles to the main building, frequently at a lower pitch to allow it to fit below the eaves level. Separate ancillary buildings may help to enclose space in front of the house by projecting forward, or they may act as extensions, following and continuing the roof line at a lower level.

Single-storey cottage at Ballyconneely, Co. Galway.

Traditional forms in the Coastal Landscape

Conspicuous buildings in coastal areas are sometimes unavoidable. The form therefore takes on a special significance, as it changes the landscape and often becomes a focal point for the eye.

The earliest and still the best examples are the traditional thatched coastal cottages of the western seaboard. Even on the flattest sites they are set into the landscape, their blank gables presenting themselves as defence from the prevailing wind. The thatch tails off at the gable-end or is protected by the edge. The ridge is rounded, the soffits also to reduce suction from the wind. The thatch is often roped and tied down. The protection is not limited to the form of the house.

Simple house form at Lettergesh, Co. Galway.

The most successful present-day forms are little changed; mainly, though not exclusively, single-storey with slated rather than thatched roof and wide frontage to create a simple long, rectangular building. Extensions and additions are generally uncomplicated flat or pitched-roof buildings attached to the original simple form.

Thus the traditional thatched cottage is the precursor and model of the present form. Centuries of evolution have created a low, almost hidden, volume invariably located to maximise shelter among the folds of landscape with minimal openings and a low, rounded aerodynamically formed roof.

Traditional thatched cottage, Sky Road, Clifden, Co. Galway.

Ancillary buildings are grouped and connected with walls to create sheltered, low-lying courtyards which complete the intuitive, aerodynamic sense of protection. The resultant form is well-defined, clustered and huddled and setting itself against the elements. Even in the most exposed locations planting helps to complete the shelter. Low shrubs and stunted trees reflect the force and direction of the wind. They are supported and helped by the form of the building, and in turn provide complementary shelter.

Slated cottage, protected by shelter planting with ancillary buildings built into the slope. Lettergesh, Co. Galway.

Later examples are sometimes unavoidably conspicuous. Their form therefore takes on a special significance, as they change and influence the landscape, becoming focal points for the eye. It is all the more important therefore that their form should be simple, agreeable and readily assimilated.

Colour of buildings has an inseparable link with form. In Connemara the almost universal white paint contrasts effectively with the landscape, and in turn the strong colours of paintwork on doors and windows give character and individuality to the buildings.

Inappropriate house type. The house appears foreign to the landscape with no shelter planting and a clutter of windows and doors which is confusing to the eye.

New Buildings

There is no reason why new buildings should not respond to these generalisations about form; of course in some respects the problems have changed.

Modern buildings are frequently larger than the cottages they replace, but their scale can be handled thoughtfully. Room-heights extending into the roof-space and use of the roof space for rooms with dormer windows or roof-windows can be very successful. The use of a deeper span may suggest a shallower pitch but it should be resisted in order to maintain an adequate slope (30-45 degrees) to the roof.

Large house kept in scale by use of roof-space and separation of volumes. Claddaghduff, Co. Galway.

The technology of trussed rafters has encouraged larger spans and lower pitches; the use of traditional collar-trusses or purlin and rafter roofs, however, allows for creative use of the roof-space, a more economical enclosure of volume and a better exterior appearance.

Building Extension

The high visibility of most buildings beside the coast makes the question of alteration and extension a central one. Against a hillside or beside the road, extensions may be discreet, but seaward-facing houses often show their 'backs' to the road, and the extension needs careful attention.

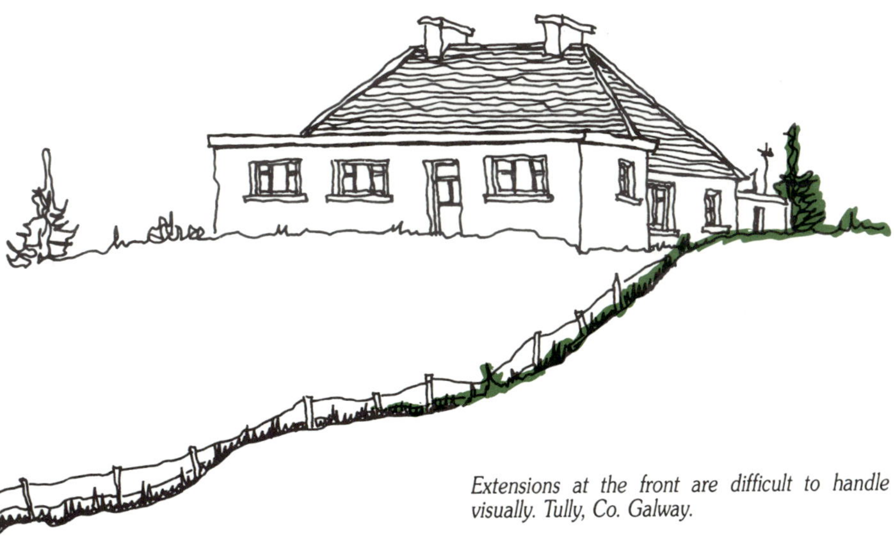

Extensions at the front are difficult to handle visually. Tully, Co. Galway.

Mobile Homes

It is little consolation that badly-sited mobile homes have only a 'temporary' effect. They should be subjected to the same principles for location as permanent dwellings, and particularly where caravan parks are involved, the questions of siting, screening and shelter are of primary importance.

Neat reception office for caravan park at Lettergesh, Co. Galway.

Building Types

The following building types cover the typical range of houses to be found in Connemara. They are not comprehensive, but are sufficient to show that there are patterns in the types of buildings which occur. They can similarly be identified and categorised for other regions.

Thatched cottage

The basic form is very simple, two or three rooms, a window to each room, stone walls and a thatched roof. The gables are blank, sometimes with small upper windows, they have a front with door and windows and a rear with door and no windows. They sometimes extend at the rear to accommodate a settle-bed.

Typically they have a central chimney, but there are larger types with more windows and chimneys. They are visibly built to resist the weather, and can still be found throughout Connemara. They are usually whitewashed, but in South Connemara the natural stone is left exposed.

Traditional thatched cottage. South Connemara.

Single-storey gable cottages

This is perhaps the most prevalent type, a derivation from the thatched cottage form, but with more generous windows, slated or tiled roof, a simple rectangular form usually with kitchen entrance extended at the rear. Built from stone and, later, blockwork, they are rendered externally and usually painted white.

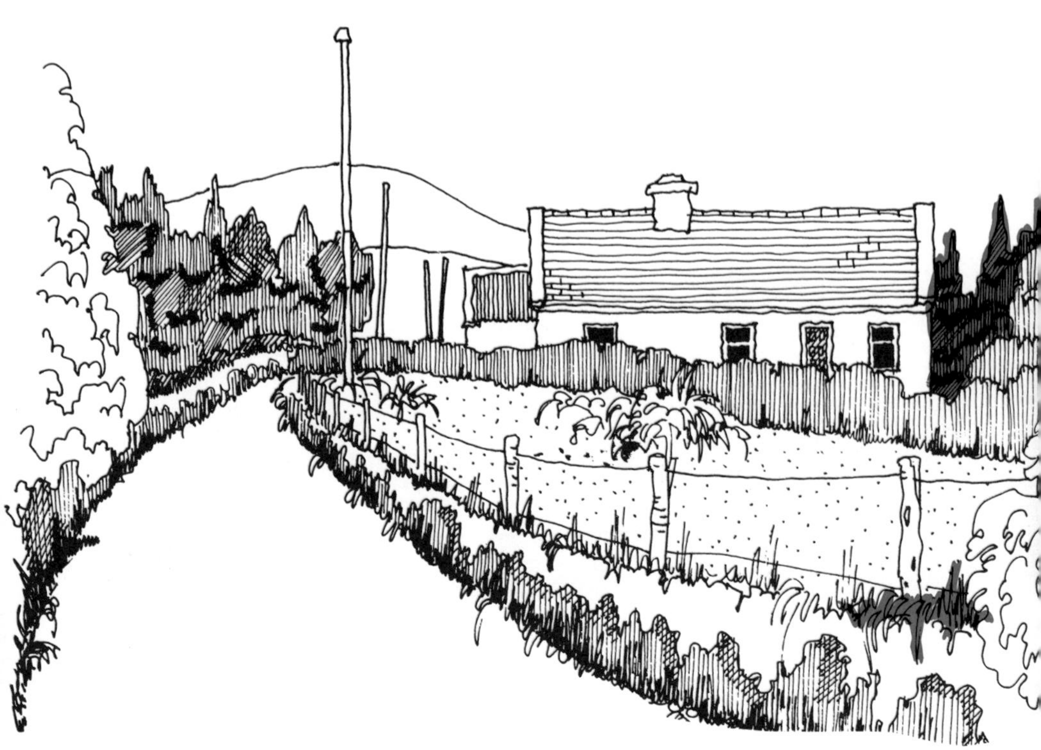

Single-storey gabled cottage at Tully Cross, Co. Galway.

Single-storey hipped-roof cottages

This is a common, standard-plan type with variations where the depth of the building is greater. The openings are symmetrical and the form is very clear.

Hipped-roof cottage at Lettergesh, Co. Galway.

Cottage-style dormer houses

This is a common two-storey solution which exploits the roof-space and keeps the scale modest. Although the dormer is a separate shape added to the house it reads as part of it because both roof and walls continue in the same materials.

Cottage-style dormer house at Tully Cross, Co. Galway.

Two-storey houses

These are not so common in Connemara. They have simple, classical proportions usually with a symmetrical facade and smaller upper windows, slated roof and whitewashed walls.

Modernised two-storey house, Lettergesh, Co. Galway.

Larger houses

For the most part these were built in the mid nineteenth century, landowners houses with extensively landscaped grounds. They used gabled dormers frequently and imposed their presence on the landscape. The tree and shrub planting have now produced mature settings which sucessfully contrast with the bleaker surroundings.

House at Moyard, Co. Galway.

Modern-day bungalow

There are so many that it is impossible to classify these. Many retain a simple gable and pitched roof form which is discreet in the landscape. However, window size, proportion and distribution are almost universally unsatisfactory; too wide, too large and overwhelming the elevation by presenting too much window relative to the solid areas. Most were designed with suburban locations in mind, and were not subsequently adapted to a rural situation. Many come from books of plans which take no account of the actual location.

Suburban bungalow in rural location. Lettergesh, Co. Galway.

Design guidelines

Twin-gabled new house well set in existing landscape. Cleggan, Co. Galway.

The form and plan of a house

Single-storey houses

Earlier forms observed were one room deep, and consequently had long frontages. All rooms faced one way with windows on one side. It is not essential to continue this as more compact plans can be achieved with rooms front and back, except where the view and sunshine requirements suggest it. However, a deeper plan gives a higher roof and requires a trussed rafter to make the longer span. To avoid the appearance of a squat, bulky form, consideration should be given to minimising the depth and incorporating some of the slope of the roof within the room. A rafter and purlin system, spanning between interior walls appears to be the simplest roof system to achieve this.

Traditional thatched cottage. Lettergesh, Co. Galway.

In summary, the following guidelines might be observed:

- *Use a single-storey form if possible in areas where single-storey houses are prevalent. It is less conspicuous in sensitive landscapes.*
- *If you use a two-storey form explore ways of reducing the exterior volume by using the roof-space for bedrooms.*
- *Make the plan longer than it is deep to avoid making a squat bulky form in the landscape.*
- *Keep the plan-form simple to maintain a clean roof-shape.*
- *Extend the house at the rear and side in preference to the front, apart from the entrance porch.*
- *Maintain the roof pitch at 45 degrees if possible, and not below 30 degrees.*

Modern holiday cottage, discreetly located and simply designed. Killary Harbour near Leenane, Co. Galway.

Two-storey houses

Two-storey buildings may be used quite satisfactorily in the landscape, but they are more conspicuous and it takes longer to grow shelter-planting. The best traditional examples are simple, classical and symmetrical in proportion. Typically they have central entrance with porch, and symmetrically placed windows on either side.

The form in Connemara is usually upright and approaching a square proportion, but many examples elsewhere have wide frontages with the width longer than the height.

An intermediate form is the dormer cottage, and most people choose either single-storey or dormer versions. Nevertheless there are situations where two-storey houses are appropriate, for example with larger houses or guest-houses and the effects of scale should be weighed against the particular location.

The form, as with single-storey, should be simple and clear. The use of gable-fronted elevations should be treated with caution, though some beautiful 19th century houses incorporate these.

Classical simplicity in two-storey house. Near Clifden, Co. Galway.

The external elements of a house

Walls and gables

The widespread use of plastered or rendered walls is the strongest guideline. In Connemara walls are almost invariably painted white, though in other regions colour is widely used. Thus the buildings are usually prominent in the landscape. In those areas where white prodominates it is better to conform or to choose very light-coloured variation.

In areas where stonework is prevalent, the buildings usually blend with the natural colours of the landscape. The use of stonework is a desirable option, but where cost precludes it, carefully chosen stone-coloured paints may be considered. However, the use of brickwork, artificial stone and features of brick and stonework cladding such as crazy paving is rarely satisfactory and should be avoided.

The discreet visual appearance of stonework might be considered where the over-riding intention is to lose the building in the landscape.

Pre-fabricated house with inappropriate windows, too many materials, low-pitched roof.

The elegant simplicity of rendered walls provides a contrast to the above.

The gable of a house looks uncomfortable if it has too many windows or openings puncturing it. On a deep plan it is often essential to place windows on the gable and sometimes doors. These should be handled very carefully to avoid the appearance of weakness of the gable. The use of a hipped roof may be considered for a deep plan, as it allows for more even puncturing of each of the sides.

In summary

- *Use materials prevalent in the area; do not mix materials such as stone and brick-work.*
- *Avoid 'feature' elements in different materials.*
- *Observe and use colours used locally on painted houses; if in doubt stick to white or light colours.*
- *Use stone if affordable in areas where stone is prevalent.*
- *Stick to small openings in the gable, away from the corner.*

Porch and gable: minimum pitch of roof (30 deg.).

Roofs

Roofing materials

Traditionally thatch, corrugated iron and slate were most commonly used. In general they look good. Corrugated iron needs maintenance and eventual painting; it is now rarely used for habitable dwellings. Thatch as a material is regrettably disappearing due to maintenance rethatching and insurance costs. Slate remains the best surface from all points of view, and asbestos-cement substitutes are now technically satisfactory. Concrete tiling is frequently used; it doesn't look as clean and weathers less well than slate. Darker colours are preferable, such as those which imitate slate colours. In Connemara, the use of slate or slate substitute lends a coherence between existing and new and should be encouraged.

Chimneys

The chimney capping and haunching now commonly used is thin in appearance. The necessary weathering could be accommodated using a block dimension below the capping to give a more solid appearance.

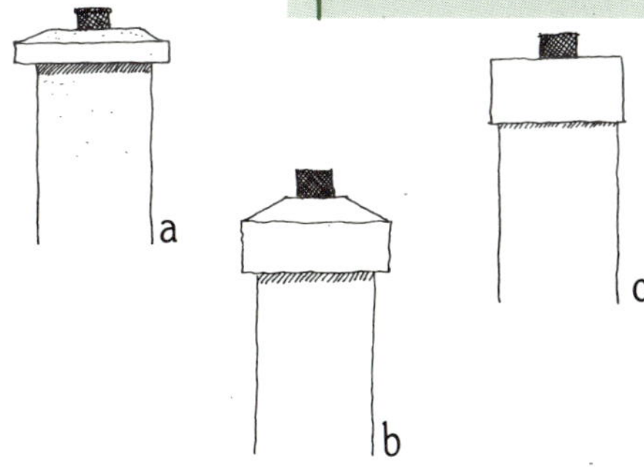

B and C are preferable to A.

Verges

It is common to build with verges and bargeboarding overhanging the gable. The roof appears to float above the house which is visually unsatisfactory, whereas the traditional way of extending the gable-wall upwards holds the roof and gives excellent protection to its vulnerable edge.

Rainwater pipes divide the elevations very strongly. It is best to bring them to the corners, or to use a light-coloured material to minimise the impact.

Dormers and roof-windows allow use of the roof-space. Gable projects above and holds the roof, dormers and roof windows.

Dormers

The value of reducing the apparent volume of a building has already been stressed. The use of dormers i.e. windows projected from the roof, provides satisfactory light for upstairs rooms under the roof and can lead to savings in overall building cost. They are most easily made in timber carcassing, then covered with lightweight cladding. The flat-roofed and timber-sheeted versions clash unhappily with the roof. It is preferable to use slate, or substitute pitched and vertical to limit the materials in use or to build as traditionally with masonry supporting walls, or with a lightweight render on mesh.

Roof-windows

Roof-windows are a new and welcome introduction to house-building. They dramatically increase flexibility in the use of the roof space and allow light into the centre of a deep plan. They do not break up the simple roof form at a distance. To retain the simple appearance they may be better located on the rear pitch of the roof.

In summary

- *Use slate if possible, or slate-substitute, or darker coloured concrete tiles.*
- *Consider the use of a traditional verge, where the gable wall goes above the roof to hold and protect it at its vulnerable edge.*
- *Use roof windows to make the most of roof-spaces.*
- *Dormers should look like an extension to the roof, using the same materials.*
- *Choose a robust, clean chimney form as the chimney silhouette is very conspicuous. The commonly-used capping is thin and looks weak.*

Entrances and porches

Entrances should express clearly their importance on the elevation, signalling obviously where the house is entered. Care should be taken to set these away from prevailing winds. This is where a porch is valuable because a door can be placed on any one of three different orientations.

Porches and extensions to the basic form are often necessary and useful to complete the plan. They should appear to be subsidiary to the main form. There are frequently difficulties with attaching secondary elements such as garages to the basic form, and low-pitch or flat-roof extensions are common. However with care it is usually possible to retain the same pitch as the main roof, and preferable. Ancillary buildings such as the garage can be used to create sheltered areas.

Glazed porches and conservatories as sun-traps can usually be added without visual problems, though they need to be robust in severe climatic conditions.

In summary

- *Keep the entrance away from prevailing winds, or use a porch.*

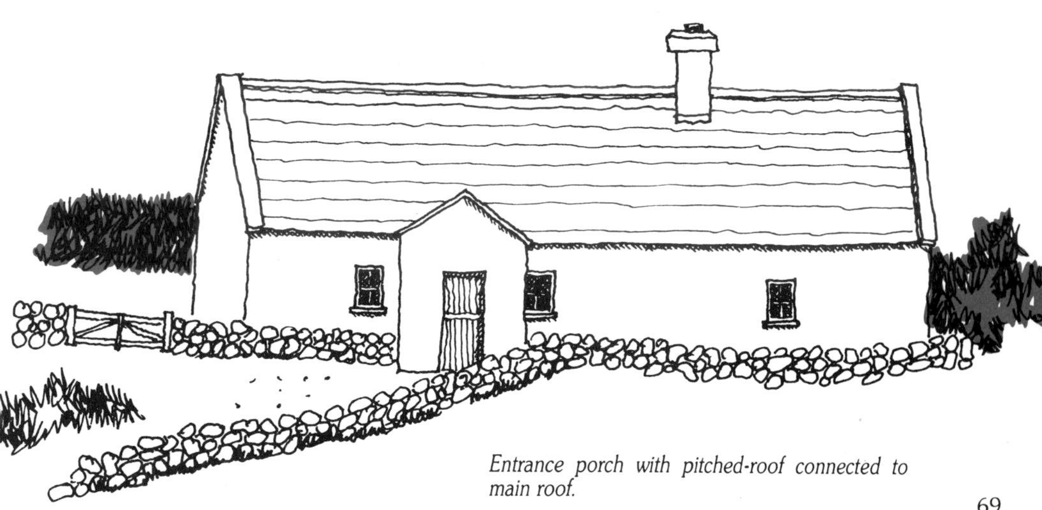

Entrance porch with pitched-roof connected to main roof.

Doors

Doors are most successful in their simplest form, that is, in sheeted or panelled timber and brightly-painted.

The door and surround often need to admit light to the hallway, but large glazed panels in doors do not always look good. A window above or beside the door, as with traditional doors, can leave the simple door intact.

A. Complicated, over-elaborate composition.

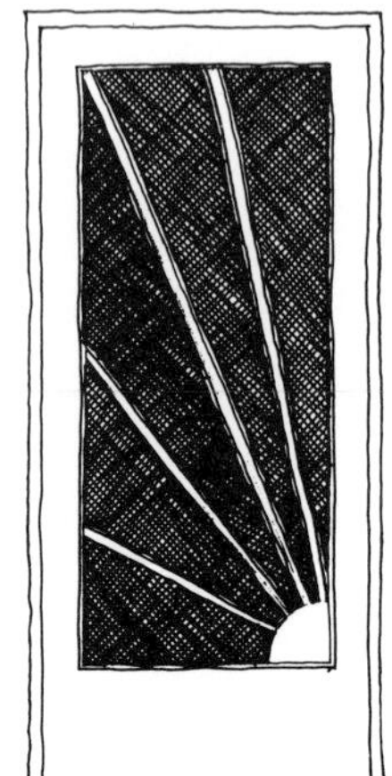

B. 'Sun burst' door.
The solid v glazing ratio is unsatisfactory.

Doors are an occasion for self-expression where the type of door and its door-knocker, letterbox and especially the paint-colour is important. But generally the 'pastiche' neo-Georgian and art-deco styles of door look out of place, as do the glazed aluminium type.

C. This type of door is commonly used today. It has a balanced composition but reduces privacy, gives little opportunity for the use of colour and can cause glare in the hallway.

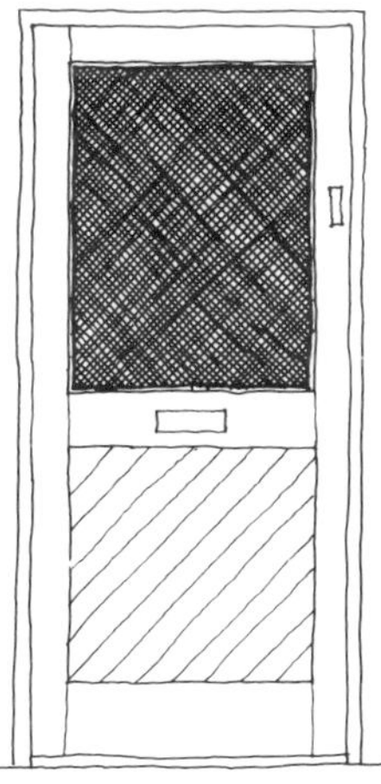

D. A version of (C) with large glazed panel above and diagonal timber boarding below. A more balanced and energy-conscious design.

E. A simple panelled door.

Windows

Windows create problems of scale and proportion. Older houses almost universally used sash windows with consistent and satisfactory proportions. Generally these were 3-4 feet wide and 5-6 feet high, with consistently narrower height than width. They occurred in the elevation with more masonry around them than window. Wider windows were used but they invariably observed the principle of subdivision to retain the scale. Present-day window choice provides an infinite range of size and proportion and great care is needed to make an appropriate selection.

Larger windows are appreciated for the view they afford, but should be used with care and avoiding proportions which are longer than they are high. Windows weaken the elevation if brought too close together or too close to the corner. A more energy-conscious approach to window design has encouraged a return to smaller windows. In some countries maximum window-size is limited for energy-conservation reasons.

In summary

- *Avoid very large windows.*
- *Use proportions which make the window higher than it is wide.*
- *Subdivide large windows to maintain those proportions.*
- *Don't locate windows too close together or too close to the corner.*

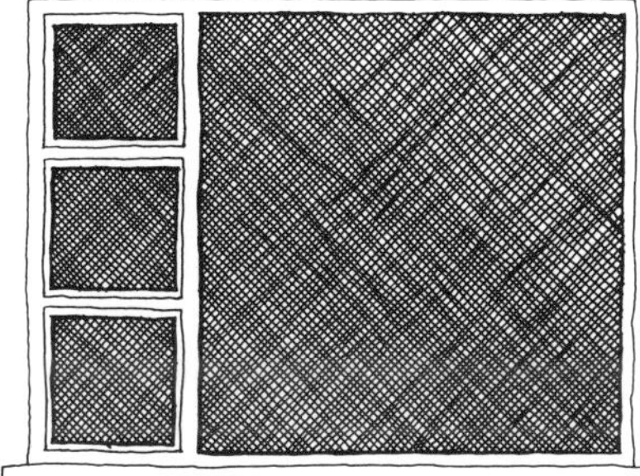

A. Living rooms may need large windows, but ones with a horizontal emphasis should be avoided.

B. A large window divided vertically is visually more satisfactory.

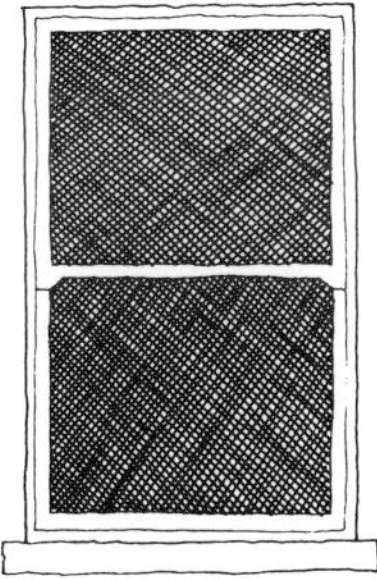

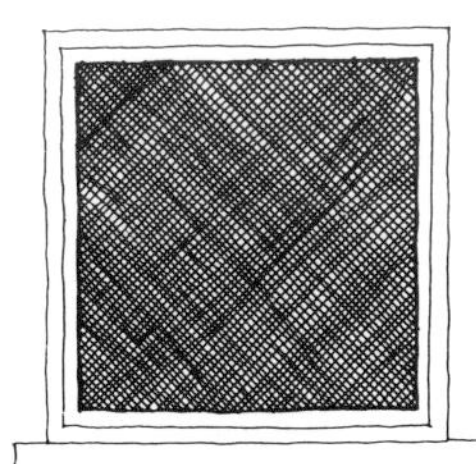

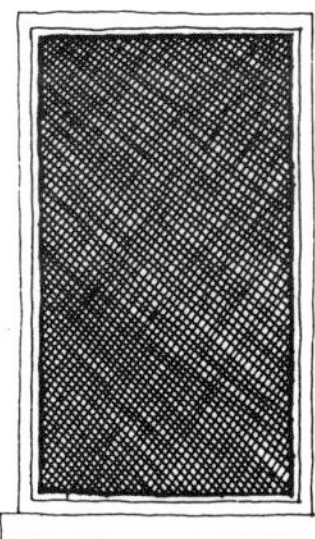

C. Smaller windows with vertical emphasis or of square proportion look more comfortable.

Colour on windows and doors

Windows and doors have always represented an opportunity for the use of colour to enliven and give individual character to the house. The combination of white-washed walls and brightly painted windows and doors is a well-loved image of Ireland, capable of infinitely varied interpretation.

White and brightly-painted woodwork looks good, suggesting that use of condensation-prone aluminium finishes and hardwood timber finishes should be discouraged.

Extensions

The flat roof extension is too universal to ignore, yet the flat roof is problematic in a severe climate, with awkward edge details. It is rarely well insulated and has difficult junctions with the ordinary roof. Therefore a pitched roof is recommended.

An extension should be discreet. It is rarely successful at the front since it spoils the original front elevation. However, a porch or minor extension can work. If possible roof and walls should reflect the existing materials.

- *Build extensions from the same materials as the house, locating them discreetly, at the rear or side if possible.*
- *Avoid flat-roofed extensions.*

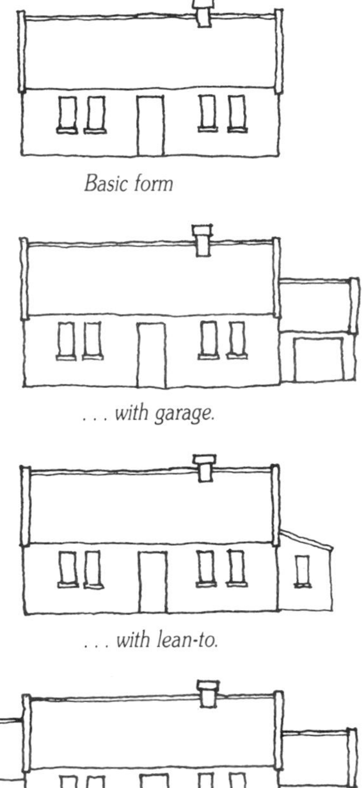

Basic form

. . . with garage.

. . . with lean-to.

. . . with extra room and garage.

. . . with two-storey extension.

The extension looks best when subsidiary to the main frame.

Services
Sewage disposal

Provision for sewage disposal by septic tank is a normal requirement in countryside location. This may affect siting insofar as space is required for the tank, the ground soakage area and the reserve ground soakage area, and there are minimum distances to be observed. The ground soakage area needs to be relatively flat. Technical requirements and advice can be obtained from the local planning authority.

Wirescape

Electrical and telephone wires and poles should be recognised as visual elements in the countryside. There are locations where the domination of the landscape with cables, wires and poles is very unsightly. Their location is rarely subjected to any landscape considerations. Routeing of both electrical and telephone wires should be made with concern about their visual impact, avoiding horizons where possible and unsightly grouping of poles. The best route is not necessarily the most direct. Even with a single house supply, careful consideration should be given to the best route from a visual point of view.

The wiring outside this house in Tully Cross is complicated and ugly. It could have been simpler. Connemara, Co. Galway.

Signs

Many roads are spoiled by indiscriminate placing of signs advertising hotels and shops. They should not be scattered along the open road. Where they may be necessary at junctions their size, colour and appearance should be controlled.

View of the post office, Cleggan, Co. Galway.

Stone walls

The use of natural stone walls in areas where they are prevalent is desirable in preference to plastered blockwork. The conservation of existing stone walls is also important and will help to root new buildings more naturally in the landscape.

Conclusion

The design guidelines do not advocate standard solutions. However, by showing the principles with which successful building has been undertaken in the past, they provide a reliable guide to the design of appropriate buildings today.

The skill, perception and imagination of a good designer will allow a creative interpretation rather than a mechanical application of principles. Thus, the acceptance of principles already evident in good building and the re-interpretation of needs and form will ensure a living, changing and continuous tradition to help towards the conservation of Ireland's remarkable resource of landscape.

Cautionary tales

'Temporary', inappropriate and obtrusive house provided as replacement for an unfit cottage.

Introduction

This section shows a few examples of development which for one reason or another might have been undertaken more sensitively. The drawings are based on real examples and similar developments can be seen in many counties of Ireland. They are illustrated in the hope that those building new houses will make efforts to avoid repetition of the same mistakes, by respecting basic principles of siting and design.

A bungalow in the valley

This bungalow opposite is fairly typical of new development and is by no means in the outrageous category. Its form is simple and it does no damage to the skyline. However, by comparison with its close neighbour it has no sense of belonging. The shallow, tiled roof with overhanging verge makes the house feel foreign. The large windows make an uncomfortable contrast, and the garage particularly looks out of scale, emphasised by a dark colour. The window proportions are too strongly horizontal. It stands starkly even though it is close to shelter planting and needs to be relieved and set into the site with planting.

It is an example which is far from extreme and which might have been corrected at design stage with careful observation or good advice. The sketch showing an alternative suggests how some of the problems might have been remedied at a design stage.

New bungalow beside old house has no sense of belonging.

Bungalow in the Valley.
Little effort has been made to adapt it to its location.

Modifications

Garage set back to create its own volume.

Windows more vertical than horizontal.

Living-room window noticeably larger for view.

Roof verges accentuated.

Roof of slate rather than tile.

Coping on chimney stacks made heavier.

Traditional stone wall used and retreats to form a larger space in front of the garage.

Shelter planting behind and beside house.

Smaller size of window reduces glare in the rooms and saves on heating costs.

Version of the bungalow with modifications.

A shop in highly scenic countryside

On one side of the road is one of the most spectacular views in Europe. On the other side of the road, an erstwhile souvenir shop dominates the view. It is a shallow-pitch corrugated-iron roof and concrete block shed, gouged into the hillside. Its windows are unnecessarily large, the entrance crudely made, the ancillary buildings are a mess and the car-parking area is a wasteland.

This building should not have been located in this situation, especially with the nearest village being only 2 miles away. Whilst its form is hardly offensive its windows and door openings are not appropriate and the total absence of landscaping highlights the bruising impact of the building.

Villages by the seaside

This first example relates to a village with a very exposed location, low-lying with a network of small roads. The houses in the village itself are relatively closely grouped around the centre and create some sense of place, but their dispersal beyond is meaningless and untidy. Houses are located very close to the sea, and in the low-lying landscape they occupy most of the horizon. The overall effect is incoherent and damaging to the landscape.

This village is located in another low-lying coastal area, where development has been intense and quite haphazard in the last two decades. Houses are widely dispersed, with dissimilar forms and an excessive range of materials. Despite the extent of the area there is no apparent structure to development.

A house beside the sea

This is an isolated house which has a strong and negative impact on the landscape. It is obstrusive by virtue of its location and form.

A house on the coast road

This area has seen extensive linear development in recent years. Some examples are good, most have been absorbed into the robust form of the landscape, but others in their form are so inappropriate that they stick out uncompromisingly. The landscape will never absorb them, like the one illustrated.

House on a beauty spot

This is an example of how a single house can detract from the landscape. The house is prominently located on the top of a hill above the waterfall. An area of outstanding scenic beauty such as this should be protected from development.

Planting for shelter

House in Lettergesh, Co. Galway.

Planting for shelter

Ireland has a higher average wind speed in winter than most other European countries and on the western seaboard the effects of exposure are compounded by the salt-laden spray carried on the sea winds.

Once shelter is provided, however, the climate can be very favourable as is shown by the world-renowned gardens of Kerry and West Cork.

Traditionally the value of shelter planting was realised. Most of our older houses in the countryside are located in sheltered positions and are surrounded by belts of trees.

Houses set in a valley and surrounded by shelter planting. Maam Valley, Co. Galway.

Today however, many houses are sited prominently and are subject to strong gales, yet there is little consideration given to shelter planting. The reason for providing it are no less compelling than before and indeed high energy costs should encourage people to consider planting for shelter a prime concern to be undertaken as soon as the house has been built. The type of suburban garden favoured by new owners is simply not sufficient to counteract the severe climatic conditions experienced in rural locations.

Where there are trees and hedgerows already existing, they should not be removed. They provide shelter and a sense of permanence and place.

Advantages of shelter planting

Hedges, groups of shrubs and trees or shelterbelts when planted near buildings have the following advantages:

- They shelter buildings from cold winds and driving rain.
- They can reduce the fuel consumption of the building by up to 20%.
- They provide privacy.
- They improve the appearance and comfort of the immediate area as a place to live and work.
- They encourage wildlife.
- They soften the hard outlines and reduce the dominant appearance of new buildings.
- They harmonise new buildings with their surroundings.
- They provide an attractive point of interest in the countryside with varying forms, colours and textures throughout the year.

Under the climatic and soil conditions of the west of Ireland, the roots of trees should not cause any damage to foundations. Problems of windblow or the blocking of gutters by leaves can be overcome by the correct choice and siting of trees.

Shelter

The main factors influencing the effectiveness of shelterbelts are:

SITING:

Shelter planting should be across the path of the wind and should be sited to make use of and improve local features of natural shelter, such as ridges and rock outcrops. Planting on ridge tops is not recommended.

House nestling into a ridge and protected from the winds by a belt of trees and hedges. Co. Galway.

PERMEABILITY:

A good shelterbelt or hedge filters the force of the wind without causing damaging turbulence.

Incorrect.

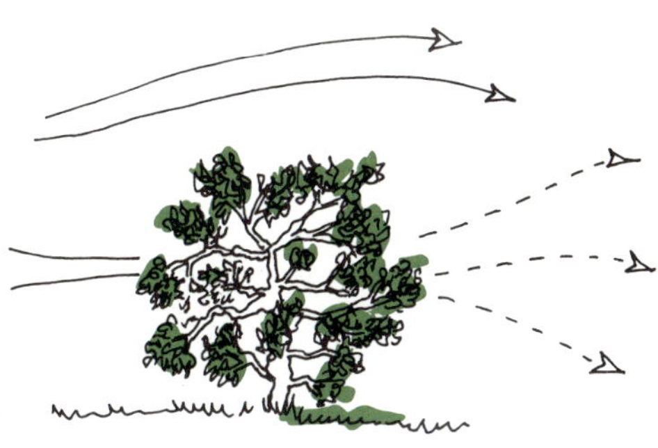

Correct.

PROFILE:

Shelter planting should lift the wind and not cause winds to be funnelled below the crown of trees. Therefore a shelterbelt should have a hedge or wind tolerant shrubs on the windward side and taller trees in the centre.

Incorrect.

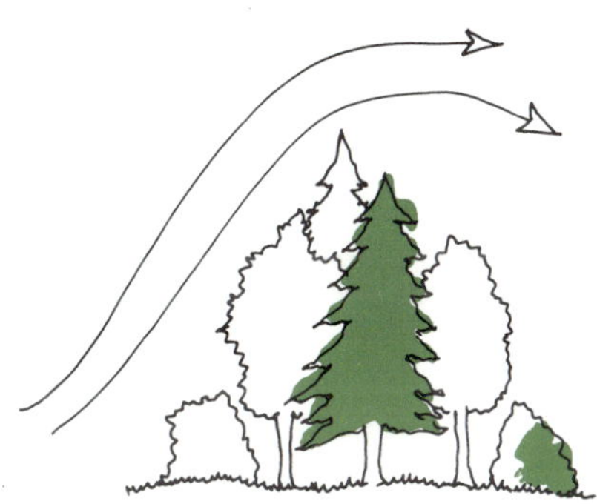

Correct.

HEIGHT AND LENGTH:

As a rule the sheltered zone will extend for a distance 20 x the height of the trees and will become effective when the length exceeds 12 x the height.

Choosing plants

Choose trees and shrubs that look right in the local landscape. Those commonly found in hedges and woods are best, although exotic shrubs such as fuschia, hebe and daisy-bushes are now part of the western landscape.

Species should be chosen for the local soil and drainage conditions. For example rhododendrons will not grow on limey soils and many species will not tolerate waterlogged conditions.

Planting

A shelterbelt should consist of not less than three rows of trees with a row of broadleaved trees included, together with a hedge. Forestry transplants or 'whips' up to 18" (500mm) tall should be pit planted at 2m spacings in staggered rows. In very exposed conditions planting should be on the leeward side of a stone wall, dyke or timber lath screen.

Stock-proof hedges should be purely hawthorn, with plants 9"-18" (250-500 mm) high at 9" (250 mm) spacing in a double staggered row 6" (150 mm) apart, giving eight plants per metre.

Purely amenity hedges may contain other species as well as hawthorn and may be planted in a single row at 12" (300 mm) spacing.

Aftercare

Trees and shrubs should be well watered after planting and hedgerow shrubs cut back to 4" (100 mm) above ground to encourage bushy growth.

Plants cannot compete for water with a mat of grass or weeds. The soil should be kept clean with mulch, herbicides or black polythene.

Larger trees may need a short stake, about 1 m tall, to hold the roots until established and should be removed in the second year.

Further reading

Conservations and Amenity Advisory Service leaflets on Tree Planting in the Countryside, Hedgerow Management and Weed Control.

Free with S.A.E. from:
An Foras Forbartha,
St. Martin's House,
Waterloo Road,
Dublin 4.

Suitable species

In exposed coastal areas the following are the species likely to succeed and are selected for their tolerance to salt-laden winds. However, there are places on the west coast of Ireland where conditions are too severe for the growth of trees or shrubs.

Species	*Common Name*	*Evergreen*	*Height (ft)*	*Rate of Growth*
Acer pseudoplatanus	Sycamore		60	F
Alnus glutinosa	Alder		35	F
Atriplex halimus portulacoid	Tree purslane	S	6	M
Crataegus monogyna	Hawthorn		25	M
Eleagnus macrophylla pungens	Oleaster	*	12	M
Escallonia macrantha		*	10	F
Euonymus japonicus	Spindle	*	15	M
Fraxinus excelsior	Ash		60	F
Fuschia magellanica	Fuschia		8	F
Griselinia littoralis		*	15	F
Hebe brachysiphon		*	6	M
Hippophae rhamniodes	Sea buckthorn		8	M
Ilex aguifolium	Holly	*	25	S
Olearia macrodonta	Daisy bush	*	15	F
Olearia traversii			20	VF
Pittesporum tenuifolium		*	15	F
Picea sitchensis	Sitka spruce	*	100	VF
Pinus nigra maritima	Corsican pine	*	120	M
Pinus pinaster	Maritime pine	*	100	F
Pinus radiata	Monterey pine	*	120	F
Populus alba	White poplar		70	VF
Prunus spinosa	Blackthorn		10	F
Quercus ilex	Holm oak	*	50	M
Salix alba	White willow		90	VF
Sambucus nigra	Elder		12	F
Senecio greyii		*	3	
Sorbus intermedia	Whitebeam		50	F
Tamarix		*	10	M
Ulex europaeus	Gorse	*	8	

Planning Authorities

The thirty-two major authorities in Ireland where planning applications are processed are listed here. By applying the principles outlined in this book you can be sure of a sympathetic and helpful hearing from your planning authority subject to local development plan considerations.

Clare County Council,
The Courthouse,
Ennis, Co. Clare.

Carlow County Council,
County Offices,
Carlow.

Cavan County Council,
The Courthouse,
Cavan.

Cork County Council,
County Hall,
Carrigrohane Road, Cork.

Cork Corporation,
City Hall,
Cork.

Donegal County Council,
County House,
Lifford, Co. Donegal.

Dublin Corporation,
Block 2, Irish Life Centre,
Lower Abbey Street, Dublin 1.

Dublin County Council,
Block 2, Irish Life Centre,
Lower Abbey Street, Dublin 1.

Galway Corporation,
Corporation Offices,
Prospect Hill, Galway.

Galway County Council,
County Buildings,
Prospect Hill, Galway.

Kilkenny County Council,
John's Green,
Kilkenny.

Kildare County Council,
St. Mary's,
Naas, Co. Kildare.

Kerry County Council,
Thomas Ashe Hall,
Tralee, Co. Kerry.

Laois County Council,
County Offices,
Portlaoise, Co. Laois.

Limerick Corporation,
City Hall,
Limerick.

Limerick County Council,
County Buildings,
80/83 O'Connell Street, Limerick.

Leitrim County Council,
The Courthouse,
Carrick-on-Shannon, Co. Leitrim.

Longford County Council,
County Offices,
Longford.

Louth County Council,
County Offices,
Dundalk, Co. Louth.

Mayo County Council,
The Courthouse,
Castlebar, Co. Mayo.

Meath County Council,
County Hall,
Navan, Co. Meath.

Monaghan County Council,
County Offices,
Monaghan.

Offaly County Council,
The Courthouse,
Tullamore, Co. Offaly.

Roscommon County Council,
The Courthouse,
Roscommon.

Sligo County Council,
Riverside,
Sligo.

Tipperary County Council (NR),
The Courthouse,
Nenagh, Co. Tipperary.

Tipperary County Council (SR),
Emmett House,
Clonmel, Co. Tipperary.

Waterford County Council,
Arus Brugha,
Dungarvan, Co. Waterford.

Waterford Corporation,
City Hall,
Waterford.

Westmeath County Council,
Mullingar,
Co. Westmeath.

Wexford County Council,
Spawell Road,
Wexford.

Wicklow County Council,
County Buildings,
Wicklow.